Original title:
Frolic in the Dreamy Fields

Copyright © 2024 Creative Arts Management OÜ
All rights reserved.

Author: Julian Prescott
ISBN HARDBACK: 978-9916-90-508-1
ISBN PAPERBACK: 978-9916-90-509-8

Childhood Reveries Beneath the Oak

Beneath the oak, we'd laugh and play,
Our time a treasure, bright and gay.
Whispers of dreams in branches high,
Dancing shadows beneath the sky.

Adventures sparkled in our eyes,
Each secret shared was a sweet surprise.
The world was ours, a vast, fair land,
Together forever, hand in hand.

Sun-Dappled Dreams and Late Afternoon Sighs

In sun-drenched fields, we chased the light,
Our laughter echoed, pure delight.
Golden rays kissed our freckled skin,
Each moment woven with joy within.

As shadows lengthened, whispers grew,
The day would fade, but dreams held true.
With every sigh, a wish took flight,
In the warmth of the fading light.

The Magic of the Wandering Cloud

A cloud drifts by, so soft and white,
Adrift in dreams, it takes to flight.
I chase it softly with eager eyes,
Imagining lands beneath the skies.

It shifts and sways with a gentle grace,
Carrying secrets to a hidden place.
Through azure realms, my spirit soars,
In the dance of the skies, my heart explores.

Echoing Giggles Amidst the Glades

In tranquil glades, where laughter flows,
We wove our dreams with fairies and prose.
Echoes of giggles, sweet and light,
Chasing the shadows of fading night.

Each whispered tale, a magic thread,
In verdant nooks, where our spirits led.
With every turn, our joy unconfined,
In the heart of the woods, pure bliss we find.

The Language of the Butterflies

Whispers in colors dance through the air,
Soft wings flutter, secrets to share.
A gentle breeze carries tales anew,
In gardens where dreams and butterflies flew.

They sip from blossoms, sweet nectar found,
Each flutter a story, a vibrant sound.
In warm sunlight's glow, they play and they weave,
In nature's soft arms, they laugh and believe.

Starlit Adventures in the Orchard

Under the canvas of a midnight sky,
The orchards awaken, a glimpse passing by.
Fruits hang like jewels, soft glints on the trees,
Whispers of laughter swirl in the breeze.

Frogs serenade from the shadows nearby,
While fireflies dance, twinkling bright like the sky.
Each step is a story, each rustle a dream,
In starlit adventures, we wander and gleam.

Playful Breezes and Fluttering Hearts

Across the meadow, the breezes play,
With every gust, they chase clouds away.
Hearts flutter softly like leaves in the air,
As nature's sweet tunes sing without a care.

Skies blush with gold, as daylight surrenders,
To dusk's tender kiss, where wonder remembers.
Together we'll dance, leave our worries behind,
In playful embraces, our spirits entwined.

A Mosaic of Nature's Embrace

In the heart of the woods, colors unfold,
A tapestry woven with stories untold.
Each leaf a whisper, each petal a sigh,
A mosaic of moments that brush by and fly.

Rivers compose melodies, sweet and pure,
While mountains stand guard, steadfast and sure.
In nature's embrace, every breath sings,
Creating a symphony of life's simple things.

Adventures in the Waking Daydream

In the land where shadows play,
Thoughts dance like a gentle sway,
Colors blend in vibrant hues,
Every moment breathes the muse.

Eyes closed tight, I wander far,
Chasing whispers, bright as stars,
Time dissolves in endless flight,
Lost in dreams till morning light.

Voices of the Wind Through Soft Meadows

Softly calling through the glade,
Wind carries songs that never fade,
Rustling leaves in breezy cheer,
Nature's symphony is clear.

Each blade sways with gentle grace,
Whispers found in nature's face,
Echoes travel, hearts embrace,
In this vast, enchanted space.

Joy Unfurling Like Petals at Dawn

Awake in hues of morning light,
Petals bloom, a wondrous sight,
Joy unfolds without a sound,
In each corner beauty's found.

Sunrise paints the skies anew,
Golden rays in every view,
Laughter dances on the breeze,
Nature's gift, our hearts appease.

Whispers of a Golden Meadow

In a meadow rich and wide,
Golden grasses gently glide,
Whispers float on softened air,
Secrets held beyond compare.

Dancing daisies greet the sun,
Here, the world and I are one,
Every moment sings of peace,
In this place, my worries cease.

Heartbeats of Flora on the Horizon's Edge

Whispers of petals in sweet twilight,
Sunset paints the blooms in golden light.
Every heartbeat echoes the soft sigh,
Nature's embrace as the day waves goodbye.

Stars awaken, cradling the night,
Each flower's secret takes graceful flight.
Dancing shadows in the starlit breeze,
Heartbeats of flora, bending the trees.

Tender Footprints on Dew-Kissed Grass

Footprints linger where morning light glows,
Each blade of grass, in silence, knows.
Dewdrop jewels on a soft, gentle sigh,
Whispers of secrets beneath the sky.

Paths untold where the wildflowers bloom,
Sweet fragrances drift, dispelling the gloom.
In the quiet moments, spirits will dance,
Tender footprints, a new dawn's romance.

The Serene Path of Playful Secrets

A winding trail where laughter hides,
In the rustle of leaves, playful guides.
Each step unfolds a story untold,
Serenity's charm in the sunlight's gold.

Whispers of children in meadows so wide,
Chasing the breezes, with joy as their side.
In the heart of the forest, memories play,
The serene path carries them joyfully away.

Magic in the Laughter of Blossoming Times

In the air, a melody softly sways,
Laughter unfurls as the sunlight plays.
Petals whirl in a vibrant dance,
Magic unfolds in each fleeting glance.

Every fragrance, a story anew,
Blossoming dreams in the fresh morning dew.
Echoes of joy in the festival's chime,
Magic surrounds, in the laughter of time.

Secrets Hidden in the Garden

Whispers linger in the leaves,
Colors dance among the trees.
Petals hide beneath the shade,
Secrets woven, memories made.

Silent blooms and shadows play,
In the quiet, dreams sway.
Nature's pulse, a gentle call,
Offering comfort, embracing all.

Softly buzzing, bees still hum,
Echoes of the past become.
Rooted tales in every sprout,
Life unfolds, hiding doubt.

Moonlight spills on dewy grass,
Time moves slow as moments pass.
Every corner, every glade,
Holds the secrets softly laid.

A Daydream on the Hillside

Clouds drift lazily above,
Whispers of the breeze, like love.
Fields of gold, a vibrant hue,
Drifting thoughts of me and you.

Butterflies in the sunlight dance,
In this moment, we take a chance.
Carefree laughter fills the air,
With every heartbeat, we declare.

Rolling hills and distant trees,
The world fades, a sweet release.
Every blade of grass agrees,
In this daydream, minds find peace.

As shadows lengthen, twilight glows,
Echoes of the heartbeats flow.
In this place where dreams reside,
We find solace, side by side.

Soft Murmurs of the Evening Wind

Whispers brush against the night,
Stars above, a gentle light.
Crickets sing in harmony,
Nature's song, a symphony.

Waves of shadows softly creep,
In the stillness, secrets keep.
Moonlit paths where moments blend,
In the twilight, dreams ascend.

Cool caress of breezy sighs,
Closing eyes with whispered lies.
Memories drift with the stars,
Softly touched, they leave their scars.

As the night unfolds its spell,
Stories hidden, and tales to tell.
In the refuge of the night,
Soft murmurs bring the heart's delight.

Petals on the Water's Edge

Delicate blooms float and sway,
Currents trace where soft winds play.
Colors blush, reflections gleam,
Nature's brush, a painter's dream.

Ripples dance beneath the light,
Each petal glistens, pure and bright.
Stories told by each cascade,
In their journey, life portrayed.

Gentle touches grace the shore,
Carried whispers, evermore.
With every wave, a promise made,
In the stillness, love conveyed.

Drifting slowly, time stands still,
Nature's pulse, a beckoning thrill.
In this moment, hearts align,
Petals resting, yours and mine.

Harmonies of Beauty on the Horizon

Golden rays dawn on the sea,
Whispers of warmth embrace the day.
Birds dance high, wild and free,
Songs of nature in sweet ballet.

Clouds drift softly, a gentle sigh,
Painting hues of pink and blue.
Here, time wanders, moments fly,
A canvas alive, vibrant and true.

Mountains rise, strong and grand,
Guardians of dreams that never fade.
In their shadows, we take a stand,
Chasing the beauty the world has made.

Harmony sings in every heart,
Echoing softly through the trees.
In each corner, a brand new start,
Beauty flows like a gentle breeze.

Enchantment Under the Blooming Willows

Beneath willows, whispers hum,
The ground is soft, a carpet green.
Sunlight filters, shadows come,
In this place, magic can be seen.

Flowers blush, with colors bright,
Petals dance, twirling in glee.
Softly they sway in the soft light,
Sharing secrets with the breeze.

Rippling waters sing their song,
Mirroring dreams, daydreams unfold.
Each moment here feels so strong,
Time remembers, stories told.

Under branches, hearts entwine,
Every breath, a sweet delight.
In this haven, all is fine,
Lost in wonder, day turns to night.

A Journey Through Forgotten Petals

In gardens wild where dreams once lay,
Petals whisper tales of old.
Each color sings of yesterday,
Secrets of love and pains untold.

Footsteps soft on paths of dew,
Every leaf a story's thread.
Nature holds what once was true,
Memories bloom where shadows tread.

Time flows like rivers, deep and wide,
Carrying wishes on its tide.
Through forgotten blooms, we will glide,
In this journey, our hearts abide.

As twilight falls, the stars ignite,
Guiding us through the night's embrace.
In this moment, pure and bright,
We find solace in this space.

Beneath the Wildflower Sky

A tapestry of blooms unfolds,
Colors bright in wild display.
Nature's canvas, stories told,
Underneath the vast blue sway.

Whispers float on a gentle breeze,
Carrying scents of earth and sun.
In this moment, hearts find ease,
In the dance of life, we're one.

Clouds drift by, a slow parade,
Dreams take flight on wings of air.
In this beauty, worries fade,
Our souls merge with the world laid bare.

With twilight's grace, the stars appear,
Beneath this sky, we find our song.
In wildflowers, love draws near,
Where every heart can truly belong.

Pockets of Joy Beneath the Blooming Sky

In the meadow where daisies sway,
Gentle whispers call the day.
Breezes dance with fragrant cheer,
Sunlight glimmers, warm and clear.

Laughter bubbles under blue,
Each moment feels fresh and new.
Clouds like cotton, drifting by,
Dreams take flight beneath the sky.

Children play in joyful spree,
Nature wraps them, wild and free.
Every smile a treasure found,
Magic pulses through the ground.

Underneath the arching trees,
Joy is carried on the breeze.
Beneath blooms of bright delight,
Hope and wonder ignite the night.

Secrets Hidden in the Green Haven

In the forest, shadows weave,
Whispers of the leaves believe.
Secrets held in every bough,
Rustling tales, a solemn vow.

Mossy carpet plush and deep,
While the old trees softly sleep.
Footprints of the deer align,
Nature's canvas, pure design.

Beneath the ferns, the world hides,
Where the tranquil spirit bides.
Sunbeams pierce the emerald veil,
Telling stories soft and frail.

Hidden paths in green embrace,
Leading to a secret space.
Time stands still in twilight's glow,
Where the heart learns how to flow.

The Playful Echo of Laughter's Drift

In the park where children play,
Echoes of joy fill the day.
Balloon colors soar on high,
As giggles chase the soft blue sky.

Swing sets creak, a rhythmic song,
Each moment sweet, where hearts belong.
Playful shouts, a gentle breeze,
Joyful chaos, time to seize.

Carousel spins, bright lights glow,
Memories made, a lovely show.
Whispers carried on the wind,
Unity in laughter, we find.

As the sun begins to fade,
Promises of joy cascade.
The playful echo lingers long,
In our hearts, forever strong.

Unruly Dreams in the Gentle Wind

In the twilight where shadows play,
Dreams take flight and drift away.
Whispers of the night entice,
Beneath the stars, a world so nice.

Winds of change swirl all around,
Carrying thoughts that are unbound.
Every hope, a kite in flight,
Caught between the day and night.

On this journey, hearts will soar,
Chasing visions from the core.
Imagination paints the scene,
A canvas lush, a vibrant green.

Unruly dreams, like waves, collide,
Guided by the currents wide.
In the gentle wind we trust,
To chase the dreams, as dreams we must.

The Bright Horizon of Daydreams

In the morning light, I drift away,
Chasing whispers of dreams that play.
The sky a canvas, painted bright,
Each color a wish, taking flight.

With every breath, a story unfolds,
In the realm where hope beholds.
Clouds like cotton, soft and free,
Bathe my soul in tranquility.

The sun spills gold on the waking earth,
Reminding me of my own worth.
As day awakens, I rise, I soar,
In the bright horizon, I yearn for more.

Finding joy in the moments that tease,
Dancing light on branches, swaying trees.
Embracing the magic, I sway and spin,
For in daydreams, life begins within.

A Tangle of Thoughts Among the Violets

Amidst the blooms, my mind does weave,
Tangled thoughts that never leave.
With violets nodding, secrets sway,
In gardens where fairies come out to play.

Petals whisper stories aged,
Of love and loss, their wisdom paged.
In every crease, in every line,
A memory lingers, sweet as wine.

The sun dips low, a golden hue,
Casting shadows where dreams construe.
In this maze of fragrant delight,
I chase the dusk, my heart takes flight.

Nature cradles thoughts unspoken,
In the tangled path, my heart is broken.
Yet among the violets, I find my way,
To mend the seams, to greet the day.

Wandering Heart in Nature's Embrace

Upon the trail where silence breathes,
A wandering heart, lost beneath the leaves.
With every step, the world unfolds,
In nature's arms, a tale retold.

Mountains rise to touch the skies,
While rivers sing their lullabies.
Soft moss cushions paths of green,
Where all is pure, serene, unseen.

In the whispering woods, I pause to feel,
The heartbeat of earth, the pulse so real.
In every rustle, in every sigh,
A promise kept beneath the sky.

With sunlit paths and moonlit dreams,
This wandering heart knows what it seems.
In nature's embrace, I lose the fight,
And find my soul in the starry night.

Twilight's Kiss on the Open Field

When twilight drapes its velvet cloak,
The world transforms, as shadows soak.
Fields of gold, now touched by night,
Embrace the sky with fading light.

A gentle breeze begins to play,
Caressing the thoughts of the day.
In this hour of whispered dreams,
Reality fades, or so it seems.

Stars awaken in a shimmering daze,
Painting stories in their glowing gaze.
The moon above casts silver streams,
Dancing softly on the seams.

In the open field, I stand amazed,
Wrapped in twilight's tender haze.
With every sigh, a wish takes flight,
In this embrace of calm and light.

Tales Told by the Whispering Wind

Beneath the ancient trees that sway,
The wind whispers secrets of yesterday.
It carries the tales of lovers lost,
And dreams that linger, no matter the cost.

Through valleys deep and mountains high,
The breeze shares stories as it sighs.
Of battles fought and victories won,
And laughter shared beneath the sun.

In moonlit nights, it softly plays,
A melody of bygone days.
Each rustle of leaves, a gentle call,
Reminds us that time embraces all.

So listen closely, you'll find it true,
The wind has whispers meant for you.
In every gust, a piece of lore,
Tales told by the wind forevermore.

Golden Hours and Pastel Hues

As daylight fades, the colors blend,
Golden rays begin to wend.
A canvas brushed with soft delight,
Pastel hues adorn the night.

In gardens where the blossoms sway,
The sun bids farewell to the day.
Orange and pink in delicate streams,
A painter's palette woven with dreams.

The sky a tapestry, rich and vast,
Holding moments that forever last.
Each twilight spark, a gentle muse,
In golden hours and pastel hues.

As stars awaken, soft and bright,
The world transforms with the night.
But echoes of color remain anew,
In whispers of gold, in shades of blue.

The Dance of Shadows and Sunlight

In morning's glow, the shadows play,
As sunlight breaks the dawn of day.
They twirl and leap in vibrant hues,
A dance that whispers of old news.

Beneath the trees, the patterns shift,
A fleeting gift, a gentle lift.
With every step, they intertwine,
In rhythms soft, like aged wine.

As daylight wanes, the shadows creep,
In twilight's hands, secrets seep.
They cling to walls, embrace the ground,
In a world where magic can be found.

The sun bids adieu, the shadows flee,
But in their hearts, they hold the key.
To moments shared, in light's embrace,
The dance of shadows, a timeless grace.

A Flutter of Wings Above the Meadow

A flutter of wings, a gentle breeze,
In the meadow, among the trees.
Butterflies swirl in a graceful flight,
Painting the day with colors bright.

They dance on petals, soft and sweet,
As flowers bow in their rhythmic beat.
Nature's wonder in every glide,
A symphony where dreams reside.

In sunlight's warmth, they play and twirl,
A ballet of beauty in a swirling whirl.
The world awakens, alive and new,
In every flutter, a moment true.

So pause a while, let your heart see,
The charm of wings in the sunlit spree.
For in each flutter, joys unfurl,
A flutter of wings, our hearts they whirl.

Where Time Surrenders to Blissful Wanderings

In meadows rich where wildflowers sway,
The whispers of breezes gently play.
Footsteps soft on the path unwind,
In moments paused, pure joy we find.

Golden light through branches streams,
We chase softly woven dreams.
Time stands still, a fleeting glance,
As nature calls us to its dance.

With every step, the world unfolds,
Through tales of wonders yet untold.
The heart beats free, the spirit flies,
In blissful wanderings under skies.

Where laughter mingles with the air,
In the sacred silence, we find care.
Together here, our souls ignite,
Where time and bliss blend pure delight.

The Curious Call of Nature's Lullaby

In twilight's hush, the crickets sing,
A symphony of the night they bring.
Soft rustling leaves, a gentle sigh,
The curious call of nature's lullaby.

Moonlight dances on the stream,
Casting shadows that softly beam.
A world awakens, wild and free,
In the lull of night, we cease to be.

Stars sprinkle dreams across the sky,
As whispers of the night draw nigh.
Each note a promise, soft and clear,
Nature's embrace, forever near.

In stillness deep, we find our rest,
Cradled in beauty, truly blessed.
The curious call, a soothing grace,
In nature's arms, we find our place.

Echoes of Delight in Fields of Gold

As sunlight spills on amber waves,
Each golden stalk, the heartbeat saves.
In laughter's echoes, joy takes flight,
In fields of gold, the heart feels light.

The breeze it dances, whispers low,
Through rippling grains, a tender flow.
With arms wide open, we embrace,
The magic found in this sweet space.

Time drifts gently like clouds above,
Wrapped in warmth, a touch of love.
The world unfolds in hues so bold,
In harmony, the stories told.

Each step a treasure, memories made,
In fields of gold, where dreams cascade.
Together here, let laughter roll,
As we weave echoes, heart and soul.

Sunshine and Shadows in a Tangle

Beneath the sun, the shadows play,
A dance of light throughout the day.
With every step, they twist and turn,
In a tapestry of warmth, we learn.

The branches stretch, the leaves embrace,
In this charming, tangled space.
A fluttering song, a breeze's call,
In sunshine's arms, we feel it all.

Footprints linger on the ground,
As laughter spins, sweet sounds abound.
In the play of light, we find our way,
Through tangled paths, both bright and gray.

Each moment woven, rich and bold,
In sunshine and shadows, stories unfold.
Together we dance in the gentle sway,
Embracing life, come what may.

The Serenade of Wildflowers

In meadows wide, where colors bloom,
The wildflowers dance to nature's tune.
A gentle breeze whispers their song,
In this realm, we all belong.

Petals painted with hues so bright,
Softly waving in the golden light.
Their fragrance drifts on the morning air,
A melody sweet, both tender and rare.

Beneath the sky, so vast and clear,
The serenade calls those who hear.
With every step on this fertile ground,
The song of the wildflowers resounds.

Together we wander, hand in hand,
Through fields of grace, so wild and grand.
In every bloom, a story untold,
A tale of beauty, forever bold.

Sunlit Paths Through Gentle Grasses

With morning light, the path awakes,
Soft whispers flow where daylight breaks.
In gentle grasses, shadows play,
A tranquil journey, come what may.

Each step unfolds a world anew,
Where sunlit beams kiss drops of dew.
A dance of colors, swaying free,
In nature's arms, just you and me.

The rustling leaves sing nature's song,
As we meander, where we belong.
Beneath the sky, so warm and wide,
The sunlit paths our hearts confide.

Through emerald fields, our spirits soar,
In every moment, we seek for more.
With laughter bright, we leave our cares,
Beneath the sun, a love that dares.

Dreams Swaying on the Breeze

Like whispers soft, our dreams take flight,
They sway on breezes, soft and light.
In twilight's glow, they find their way,
A canvas painted at the end of day.

With every breath, we chase the stars,
In silent hopes, we heal our scars.
Time flows gentle, like the streams,
Carrying forward our cherished dreams.

Through moonlit nights, we find our peace,
In dreams, our worries gently cease.
With open hearts, the night unfolds,
In every heartbeat, new tales are told.

We'll follow paths where wishes roam,
In every sigh, we find our home.
Tomorrow's light, a brand-new chance,
As dreams sway softly, we take a stance.

Enchanted Stroll Through Fields of Gold

In fields of gold, where sunlight beams,
We wander gently, lost in dreams.
Each step a whisper, soft and sweet,
In this enchanted place, we meet.

The rustling grains, a lullaby,
As golden waves blend with the sky.
Together we roam, hearts open wide,
Through nature's wonder, we take pride.

Wildflowers burst like stars at dusk,
In the evening air, we breathe and trust.
With every golden hour that shines,
Our souls entwined as love defines.

In this sacred space, time stands still,
Each moment cherished, hearts to fill.
An enchanted stroll that never ends,
Through fields of gold, our love transcends.

Meadows of Memory and Spontaneity

In fields where the wildflowers bloom,
Whispers of laughter fill the air.
Each moment blooms like a sweet perfume,
Tangled with secrets we gladly share.

Beneath the sun's warm, gentle glow,
Time dances lightly, unbound and free.
We chase the shadows, let the heart flow,
Embracing the now, just you and me.

Memories woven like threads of gold,
In every corner, stories reside.
Each echo of joy and tales untold,
In meadows of memory, we confide.

So let's wander through this sunlit land,
With spontaneity as our guide.
Hand in hand, together we stand,
In meadows where our dreams collide.

Tranquil Reflections in a Winding Stream

Beneath the quiver of weeping willows,
Gentle ripples dance on the pond.
Mirrored images of soft, quiet meadows,
In the serene embrace of dusk, we're fond.

The water flows with a soothing sound,
Whispering tales of the earth below.
In its depths, the quiet truths are found,
In tranquil reflections, life starts to glow.

Each stone tells a story of its own,
Eroded with care by nature's hand.
Here in the calm, seeds of thought are sown,
As we sit together, perfectly planned.

The sun dips low, painting skies in cream,
As shadows stretch long along the bank.
In this moment, life feels like a dream,
In a winding stream, we find our rank.

The Magic of Unplanned Adventures

On paths unknown we dare to tread,
Where maps provide no guiding light.
Every turn sparks the heart ahead,
As serendipity takes flight.

Laughter echoes through the trees,
With every step, new wonders bloom.
A hidden trail sways in the breeze,
Inviting us to leave the room.

The thrill of chance, our souls ignite,
In every twist, a joyful find.
Unfolding stories in the twilight,
As we wander, leaving cares behind.

Let's dance beneath the starlit skies,
Embrace the night, let our spirits soar.
In every surprise, a sweet surprise,
Magic awaits, forevermore.

Silhouettes of Clouds on a Gentle Breeze

In the vast domain of azure skies,
Soft clouds drift in their fleeting grace.
Whispers of dreams as the daylight dies,
Painting shadows in a tender space.

Each silhouette tells a story profound,
Of hopes and fears, like feathers in flight.
They roam the heavens without a sound,
Guiding our thoughts into the night.

With every billow, memories are cast,
Drifting softly on a gentle stream.
A moment, a memory, fleeting yet vast,
In the twilight glow, we weave our dream.

So let us linger and watch the show,
As nature displays her tranquil art.
In silhouettes of clouds, we'll know,
The beauty of life that fills the heart.

Tails of Dandelions on the Edge of Sleep

Dandelions drift in twilight's gaze,
A whisper soft, the night decays.
Their golden tails sway in the breeze,
Carrying dreams with quiet ease.

Stars blink gently, a watchful nod,
As shadows dance on the cool sod.
Petals blend in the starlit air,
Nature's lullaby, a tender prayer.

Each puff of white, a wish in flight,
Floating peacefully into the night.
A canvas painted in silver hue,
Where wishes bloom and hearts renew.

In this moment, time stands still,
As magic spins with tranquil will.
Tails of dandelions, dreams take shape,
On the edge of sleep, a sweet escape.

Petals and Clouds in Perfect Symphony

Soft petals twirl, a gentle dance,
In harmony with clouds that prance.
Colors mingle in skies so wide,
Nature's canvas, where joys abide.

A breeze whispers secrets, sweet and light,
Guiding the blossoms in pure delight.
Each flower a note, each cloud a chord,
Together they sing, a love adored.

Underneath the sun's golden glow,
Petals and clouds in a soft flow.
A serenade of beauty shows,
In every turn, the heartache goes.

With every bloom, a story to tell,
Of dreams and hopes that weave so well.
In perfect symphony, they entwine,
A world where love and light align.

Lush Adventures in a Garden of Time

In a garden where memories grow,
Lush adventures in sunlight's glow.
Each flower a chapter, vibrant and bright,
Stories unfold in the morning light.

Butterflies flutter, a colorful race,
Dancing together, a joyful embrace.
Whispers of secrets in every petal,
Time drips softly like a sweet medal.

With each winding path, a journey we find,
Lessons and laughter intertwined.
Roots reach deep, while branches sway free,
A garden of time, where hearts can be.

Here, the world melts into pure bliss,
Every moment a magical kiss.
In lush adventures, we lose our cares,
In the garden of time, a dream that dares.

Dreamscapes of a Wandering Heart

A wandering heart drifts through the night,
Chasing shadows in soft moonlight.
Dreamscapes beckon, a call so sweet,
Where the stars and whispers of secrets meet.

Each step is a dance on celestial ground,
In a world where lost things are found.
Clouds like pillows, drifting afar,
Guiding the heart towards a new star.

In twilight's embrace, stories take flight,
With every heartbeat, a spark ignites.
Through valleys of wonder, and hills of gold,
Dreamscapes unfold like tales of old.

Among the echoes of twilight's sigh,
The wandering heart learns to fly.
In every dream, a promise blooms,
In the tapestry of night, love resumes.

Serenity in the Swaying Willow

Beneath the willow's gentle sway,
The whispers tell of dreams at play.
Sunlight dances on the stream,
In nature's arms, we find our dream.

Shadows weave with golden light,
Resting hearts in sweet delight.
Leaves that shimmer, soft and low,
Guide our thoughts where rivers flow.

Time unravels, slows its pace,
In this green and open space.
With every sigh, the world retreats,
As peace, like summer, softly greets.

Underneath the sky so blue,
The willow sways, our hearts renew.
In this moment, still and kind,
We find the solace that we seek to bind.

Elysian Fields of Forgotten Memories

In fields where shadows gently sleep,
Memories swirl, both rich and deep.
Faint echoes of laughter float,
Upon the breeze, sweet tales we wrote.

Sunset glimmers, paints the sky,
Whispers of days gone idly by.
Each blade of grass a story tells,
Of love and loss in quiet spells.

Golden grains sway in the light,
Cradling dreams that take to flight.
Moments cherished, never fade,
In this realm, our joys are laid.

As stars appear, a cloak of peace,
To every heart, a sweet release.
Here in the fields, we come to roam,
In Elysian lands, we find our home.

Fluttering Hues in a Child's Pose

In a child's pose, the world feels new,
Colors burst in every hue.
The quiet joy of life unfolds,
In peace, the heart's true tale is told.

Gentle giggles fill the air,
With every breath, we strip despair.
Rainbow dreams float through the day,
In innocence, our worries sway.

A canvas bright beneath the sun,
Where laughter dances, life's begun.
The fluttering hues embrace our soul,
With every heartbeat, we become whole.

In this moment, still and clear,
The world is vast, yet we hold near.
A child's pose, a breath to stay,
In fluttering hues, we find our way.

Fields of Solitude and Starlit Wonder

In fields of solitude, I stand,
The night unfolds with gentle hand.
Stars above like diamonds gleam,
In silent space, I softly dream.

The air is rich with whispers clear,
Each breath a note for souls to hear.
Beneath the vast and endless dome,
In solitude, I find my home.

A universe so wide, so bright,
With wonders hidden in the night.
Each twinkle tells a story true,
Of hopes and fears, a life anew.

Fields of wonder call my name,
In quiet strength, a gentle flame.
Underneath the starlit sky,
In solitude, my spirit flies.

Giggling Breezes Among the Blossoms

Whispers of laughter through the trees,
Gentle movements in the warm spring air.
Petals dance softly, caught with ease,
Nature's joy sings everywhere.

Bright colors play in the golden light,
Sweet aromas linger, inviting all.
Breezes giggle, a pure delight,
In bloom's embrace, we hear their call.

Beneath the Arch of Celestial Whispers

Stars twinkle softly, secrets they share,
Moonlight bathes the earth with grace.
Night's embrace, a tapestry rare,
In silence we find our rightful place.

Galaxies swirl in a cosmic dance,
Dreamers gaze up, hearts open wide.
Hope ignites with each fleeting glance,
Beneath the vastness, we abide.

Threads of Imagination in Pastoral Bliss

Fields of green stretch far and wide,
Where dreams weave tales under the sun.
Each blade whispers secrets inside,
Nature's canvas, joys to be spun.

Colors bloom with a vibrant song,
In every corner, magic unfolds.
Here in the heart, where we belong,
Imagination's tale is told.

Joyous Ramblings of the Earth's Children

Little feet patter on the ground,
Laughter echoes in the open air.
Nature's playground, joy is found,
In every moment, without a care.

Chasing butterflies, running wild,
Hearts are light, spirits soar high.
In the sun's warmth, each carefree child,
Finds joy beneath the endless sky.

A Tapestry of Color and Light

In the dawn, hues softly blend,
Golden rays on petals lend.
A canvas stretched, the sky that glows,
Nature's art, it ebbs and flows.

Crimson clouds in twilight's hue,
Whispers of the day, anew.
Twinkling stars in velvet night,
A tapestry of color and light.

Fields of green and rivers bright,
Infinite wonders in our sight.
Every stroke, a story told,
A dance of life, a sight to behold.

In shadows deep, the world takes flight,
As day gives way to starry night.
Colors merge in one embrace,
In a tranquil, timeless space.

Wanderlust in a Pastoral Landscape

Rolling hills and fields of gold,
Where tales of wanderers are told.
Breezes carry scents so sweet,
In nature's arms, our hearts compete.

A winding path, an endless quest,
Among the blooms, we find our rest.
Mountains rise with timeless grace,
In every corner, a new face.

Sunset paints the skies with fire,
While silence stirs the heart's desire.
With every step, a new delight,
Wanderlust, our guiding light.

Stars emerge in velvet skies,
Promises of dreams arise.
In this land of rich appeal,
We chase the echoes, hearts to heal.

The Flight of the Bumbling Bee

In gardens bright, the bee does roam,
A tiny world, a blissful home.
With buzzing wings, it flits and flies,
Chasing blooms 'neath sunny skies.

Pollen dust and nectar sweet,
From flower's heart, its journey fleet.
A dance of life, a flight in glee,
All hail the bumbling bee!

Over meadows, under trees,
Whispers carried by warm breeze.
In every bloom, a taste of cheer,
Life's simple joys, always near.

As daylight fades and shadows fall,
The bee returns, heeds nature's call.
In twilight's glow, so swift and free,
A gentle hum, the bumblebee.

Meadow Lullabies at Dusk

As daylight wanes, the shadows creep,
Nature hushes, the world in sleep.
Crickets chirp their evening song,
In meadows vast, where dreams belong.

The sky, a canvas brushed with gold,
Whispers of stories yet untold.
A soft breeze sings through the trees,
Lulling hearts with gentle ease.

Fireflies dance in twinkling flight,
Stars awaken, sparkling bright.
In every corner, peace resides,
Nestled close, where magic abides.

With every breath, the night unfolds,
Warmth of dreams in silence holds.
In nature's cradle, we find our rest,
Meadow lullabies, a timeless quest.

In the Heart of Flourishing Fields

Golden petals dance and sway,
Underneath the bright green sky.
Whispers of the gentle breeze,
Nature's song, a sweetened sigh.

Colors burst in vibrant hues,
Painted by the hands of light.
Every corner, life anew,
A canvas kissed by pure delight.

Butterflies and bees at play,
Filling air with joyful glee.
In the heart of fields today,
Harmony and peace run free.

As the sun begins to set,
Casting shadows long and wide.
In these fields, we won't forget,
The beauty of this golden tide.

Flickers of Dawn Across the Open Lands

Morning light begins to creep,
Through the valleys, soft and pale.
Dewdrops glisten, secrets keep,
In the stillness, dreams unveil.

Birds take flight in joyous arcs,
Chirping songs of the new day.
Flickers of dawn ignite sparks,
Of hope in the world's ballet.

Clouds drift lazily above,
Painting skies in shades of gold.
Embracing all with warmth and love,
As nature's stories unfold.

Across the fields, the shadows wane,
And life awakens from its rest.
In the dawn, we break the chain,
To cherish every blessed quest.

Swaying Grasses and Floating Thoughts

Swaying grasses, whispering tales,
Beneath the vast and open sky.
Each soft wave, a gentle gale,
Guiding thoughts as they drift high.

Clouds above, they morph and change,
Like fleeting dreams in restless minds.
As nature's hues, they rearrange,
In a dance that softly binds.

Sunlight filters through the blades,
A tapestry of light and shade.
In this moment, life pervades,
A canvas where our hearts are laid.

Floating thoughts like butterflies,
On gentle winds, they roam so free.
In this realm where quiet lies,
We find our peace, just you and me.

A Ride on the Carriage of Imagination

Take a seat, the journey starts,
Carriage drawn by dreams divine.
Through the realms of vivid arts,
Let your spirit intertwine.

Wheels of wonder gently roll,
Past the landscapes of your mind.
Every moment, a new goal,
Where the magic weaves and winds.

Fields of starlight, oceans wide,
Mountains high that kiss the skies.
In this dreamscape, we can glide,
As the heart forever flies.

Together on this path we roam,
With every turn, a new delight.
In our thoughts, we build a home,
On the carriage, our dreams take flight.

Sketches of Serenity in Nature's Canvas

In whispers soft, the breezes play,
Gentle strokes of green and gray.
Amidst the blooms, a quiet smile,
Nature's peace resides awhile.

A babbling brook sings sweet and low,
Kissed by sunlight's golden glow.
Dappled shadows dance and weave,
In this haven, hearts believe.

Mountains rise, majestic and grand,
Embracing dreams held in their hand.
The rustling leaves tell tales untold,
Of silent wonders, brave and bold.

Under the sky, a canvas bright,
Every hue a pure delight.
In nature's arms, we find our place,
Sketches of serenity, draped in grace.

Secrets of the Ebbing Twilight

As daylight fades, the shadows creep,
The world prepares for dreams to seep.
Whispers of night, in cool embrace,
Twilight unveils its tranquil face.

Stars awaken, one by one,
Dancing softly, night's begun.
A hush surrounds, both deep and wide,
In this stillness, secrets bide.

The moon spills silver on the shore,
A silent promise, forevermore.
Mysteries wrapped in velvet deep,
In twilight's arms, the world will sleep.

Every breath a sacred vow,
To time's sweet flow, we humbly bow.
In twilight's glow, we find our way,
A canvas painted in shades of gray.

Nature's Palette at Daybreak

With dawn's first light, the world anew,
A canvas vast with every hue.
Gold and pink in soft embrace,
Nature's art, a warm embrace.

Birds take flight, their songs take wing,
Celebrating what the morn will bring.
Each petal glows, a vibrant spark,
In this moment, love ignites the dark.

The dewdrop glistens on the grass,
Whispers of life, as hours pass.
A palette rich with colors bright,
Nature awakens in pure delight.

Through every breath, the promise swells,
Of stories woven, time compels.
In morning's glow, hearts start to beat,
Nature's palette, a rhythm sweet.

Reverberations of Joy Beneath the Trees

In whispered laughter, branches sway,
Celebrating life in every way.
Sunbeams dance in playful play,
Joy resounds beneath the sway.

The leaves respond with rustling cheer,
Echoes of joy that all can hear.
In the shade, we gather near,
With every heartbeat, love draws near.

Children's giggles fill the air,
In enchanted woods, we lay bare.
Time stands still beneath the trees,
Reverberating with gentle ease.

In this haven of earthy bliss,
Every moment, a fleeting kiss.
The symphony of life's embrace,
Joy resonates in nature's grace.

Chasing Shadows Among the Clovers

In fields where clovers sway,
Whispers of the breeze play,
Shadows dance in soft delight,
Chasing dreams into the night.

Amidst the green, a secret lies,
Where sunlight meets the skies,
Footsteps tread on velvet ground,
In this haven, peace is found.

Cloaked in hues of emerald bright,
We wander softly, hearts ignite,
Every shadow tells a tale,
Of magic wrapped within the pale.

As dusk descends, we fade away,
Yet clovers bloom at end of day,
Forever chasing shadows' grace,
In this enchanted, sacred space.

Beneath the Canopy of Starry Skies

Beneath the vast, celestial dome,
We find our hearts, we call it home,
With stars like jewels in the night,
They guide our paths, our dreams ignite.

The gentle breeze caresses skin,
While constellations twirl and spin,
Whispers from the cosmos near,
A symphony we long to hear.

In the quiet, we share our fears,
A tapestry of dreams and tears,
Together we weave our story bright,
Under the magic of starlit light.

The moonlight dances on our skin,
A promise that the light won't dim,
Forever beneath this grand expanse,
We find our place, our cosmic dance.

Dance of the Dandelion Seeds

In meadows vast, where wild winds blow,
Dandelion seeds begin to glow,
With every breath, they take to flight,
A gentle waltz, a pure delight.

They swirl and twirl in open air,
Like dreams released without a care,
A fragile dance of hopes set free,
Carried away, just like the sea.

From tiny stars to distant lands,
In nature's grip, they take their stands,
Each seed a wish, a tale untold,
In life's embrace, they daringly fold.

With every gust, new journeys start,
A fleeting moment, a work of art,
In nature's hands, we find our grace,
The dance of seeds, a sweet embrace.

Echoes of Laughter in Twilight

In twilight's glow, laughter rings clear,
Echoes of joy, so sweet, so near,
Children's voices paint the air,
With dreams alight, without a care.

Beneath the trees, shadows play,
As twilight whispers, night turns gray,
Moments cherished, soft and bright,
Resounding echoes in fading light.

With every giggle, skies ignite,
Chasing the day, embracing night,
Stories spun on gentle breeze,
Memories captured among the trees.

As stars peek out to join the fun,
The laughter dances, never done,
In those echoes, our hearts remain,
A tapestry of joy and pain.

Murmurs of Nature's Play

Whispers through the trees so high,
A gentle breeze that passes by.
Flowers dance with colors bright,
Nature sings in pure delight.

Rippling streams with laughter flow,
Sunlight casts a golden glow.
Birds are chirping, soft and free,
In this land of harmony.

Clouds drift lightly, shapes to find,
A canvas vast, by dreams aligned.
Each rustling leaf, a story told,
In the arms of nature, bold.

Every shadow, every ray,
Whispers of a bright new day.
Join the symphony of the land,
Murmurs of nature's gentle hand.

A vision in Lavender and Gold

Fields where lavender blooms abound,
Golden sun spills warmth around.
A dreamer's canvas, rich and bright,
Colors melding in the light.

Hues of twilight, softly blend,
Where the sky and earth descend.
Scent of flowers fills the air,
In this vision, joy laid bare.

Moments captured, time stands still,
Heart and spirit, both will thrill.
A tapestry so blissful, bold,
Life is painted, lavender and gold.

With every breath, the beauty grows,
Nature's palette, love bestows.
In the twilight's gentle hold,
A vision true, forever told.

Lighthearted Days in Sweet Serenity

Breezes whisper through the trees,
Bringing calm, like gentle seas.
Days unfurl, so warm and bright,
Hearts embrace the purest light.

Laughter echoes, soft and clear,
Moments cherished, drawing near.
Children playing, joy displayed,
In sweet serenity, unafraid.

Nature's bounty, rich and kind,
Brings a peace that calms the mind.
Underneath the vast, blue skies,
Love and laughter, never dies.

Welcome each lighthearted day,
In the sun's warm, golden ray.
Together, we shall sing and sway,
In sweet serenity, we'll stay.

Meadows of Laughter

In the meadows, spirits rise,
Laughter dances, never lies.
Sunshine sparkles on the dew,
Nature's joy, a vibrant hue.

Children chasing, carefree play,
In the fields, they laugh and sway.
Every moment pure and bright,
Meadows gleam in morning light.

Butterflies, in colors bold,
Whisper secrets, tales untold.
Every flower, every sound,
In this haven, peace is found.

Join the chorus, let it ring,
Life's a melody we bring.
In the meadows, heart takes flight,
Where laughter meets the soft daylight.

Gardens of Hope

In the garden where dreams are sown,
Petals whisper, seeds are grown.
Colors blooming, hearts aglow,
In these spaces, hope will flow.

Sunshine kisses every sprout,
In this haven, there's no doubt.
Futures dance on gentle wings,
Life's a gift that nature brings.

Every root, a tale to share,
In the soil, love's tender care.
Gardens flourish, strong and wide,
Cultivating joy inside.

So plant your dreams and let them bloom,
In this space, love finds its room.
Gardens of hope, a cherished theme,
Where each heart can dare to dream.

Glimmers of Joy among the Tall Grass

In the meadow where sunlight plays,
Tiny dewdrops catch the rays.
Whispers of color dance in the breeze,
Nature's laughter in rustling leaves.

Butterflies flit from bloom to bloom,
Their wings a flutter, dispelling gloom.
Each gentle sway tells a story untold,
Of simple pleasures and hearts of gold.

Children's laughter echoes nearby,
As they chase the shadows that flit and fly.
A moment of peace in the world's great rush,
Glimmers of joy ignite the hush.

With every breath, the wild things share,
A secret bond, a gentle prayer.
Among the tall grass, life unfolds,
In shimmering whispers, joy beholds.

The Canvas of Dreams and Drifting Clouds

Beneath the sky, a brilliant view,
Where thoughts take flight and dreams renew.
A canvas painted with hues so bright,
Drifting clouds weave day from night.

Each stroke of breeze brings stories anew,
Of distant lands and skies of blue.
The sun dips low, a golden ball,
As day gives way and shadows fall.

Whispers of wishes float in the air,
Entrancing visions, a world to share.
In this realm where dreams are spun,
Underneath the setting sun.

With every glance, there's magic here,
A tapestry woven with joy and fear.
In the quiet moments, we find our space,
On the canvas of time, a soft embrace.

Whimsies in the Summer Air

In the heat of day, a playful light,
Frolics and dances, a pure delight.
Children run wild, their spirits soar,
Chasing the magic that summer's store.

Bubbles float up, kissing the sky,
While laughter rings out, sweet lullabies.
The scent of blossoms stirs up the past,
Moments like these, forever to last.

Skimming stones on a shimmering lake,
With every splash, a new wish to make.
Picnics under the shade of trees,
Whimsical thoughts carried on the breeze.

As fireflies blink in the evening's glow,
We gather our dreams, letting love flow.
In the summer air, we find our way,
Creating memories that forever stay.

A Symphony of Blossoms and Breeze

In gardens where fragrances waltz and twine,
Petals unfurl, a sight divine.
Colors converge in a gentle embrace,
A symphony blooms in this sacred space.

Bees hum softly, their work regarded,
In every corner, life's song is guarded.
The wind carries tales of dusk and dawn,
As blossoms sway in a whispered yawn.

Underneath the vast azure dome,
Nature's orchestra finds its home.
Notes of a breeze, sweet and free,
Compose the harmony of you and me.

With every rustle, the tale unfolds,
A tapestry woven in vibrant folds.
In the twilight glow, hearts intertwine,
A celebration of life, forever in time.

Secrets of the Glistening Stream

Beneath the willow's bending grace,
Water whispers in a soft embrace.
Shimmering jewels, tossed in the light,
Secrets flow gently, hidden from sight.

Fish dart swiftly, shadows collide,
Rippling tales of the world outside.
Mossy stones cradle stories untold,
In this quiet haven, life unfolds.

Dragonflies dance in a sunlit waltz,
Echoing nature's forgotten faults.
The stream holds magic, pure and serene,
In its flow lies the heart of the green.

As twilight descends, stars begin to gleam,
Transforming all with a silvery beam.
Secrets of water, forever they'll keep,
In the glistening stream, where dreams softly seep.

The Rhythm of the Rustling Leaves

In the autumn's breath, the leaves confer,
Whispers of wind, a soft, gentle stir.
Crimson and gold, they twirl and sway,
A dance of nature, at the close of day.

Branches creak, in a harmonious song,
Nature's chorus, where we all belong.
Each leaf a story, a moment in time,
Rustling secrets, like a sweet, silent rhyme.

The sun filters through, casting shadows wide,
Life in the forest, where mysteries hide.
Every flutter breathes a tale anew,
Of summers past and the morning dew.

In the twilight, the rustling grows still,
Under the glow of the moon's gentle thrill.
The rhythm of leaves will forever confide,
In the heart of the woods, where dreams abide.

Twilight's Embrace on the Horizon

Soft hues of orange blend with the gray,
As twilight whispers goodbye to the day.
Shadows stretch long, embracing the night,
In this still moment, everything feels right.

Clouds brush the sky with a vibrant hand,
Adorning the canvas, as day had planned.
Night beckons softly with stars in its gaze,
Twilight's embrace lingers, a warm haze.

The river reflects the sun's last caress,
Rippling with echoes of nature's finesse.
Creatures emerge from their slumbering state,
In twilight's soft glow, they patiently wait.

The horizon ignites with a magical flare,
Promises whispered in the cool evening air.
Time holds its breath, as day turns to night,
In twilight's embrace, all is calm, all is right.

Whimsical Journeys Through Verdant Valleys

In valleys so green, where dreams take flight,
Whimsical paths guide us into the light.
Laughter of streams plays beside the trees,
Every step forward floats on a breeze.

Wildflowers bloom in a riot of hues,
Painting the landscape with nature's own views.
Butterflies flitter, while sunlight cascades,
In a world rich with wonder, each memory fades.

Mountains stand guard, ancient and wise,
Whispering tales beneath vast, open skies.
Every corner holds secrets yet sprawled,
In verdant valleys where magic is called.

As twilight descends, shadows start to play,
The day's sweet adventure now fades away.
In whimsical journeys through rustic charms,
Nature's embrace lingers, enfolding us softly in arms.

Whispers of a Gossamer Breeze

In twilight's hush, soft secrets sigh,
Gossamer threads where shadows lie.
The trees confide to the gentle air,
Whispers of dreams, delicate and rare.

A fleeting touch, ethereal grace,
The breeze, a lover, in this quiet space.
Carrying tales from faraway lands,
It dances lightly, a waltz of strands.

Morning dew glistens, nature's sweet kiss,
As whispers entwine in the depths of bliss.
Each breath a promise, each sigh a hymn,
The gossamer breeze, a world so dim.

In dusk's embrace, the whispers grow bright,
Calling the stars to join in their flight.
Together they weave a tapestry wide,
Of dreams and of secrets, like waves on the tide.

Dance of the Sunlit Meadows

In meadows bright, where daisies bloom,
The sunbeams dance, chasing the gloom.
Butterflies flit on wings of delight,
Painting the air with colors so light.

The grasses sway in a joyful tune,
Under the gaze of the afternoon.
Nature's symphony, a gentle embrace,
Where every heartbeat finds its place.

Golden rays with a warm caress,
Invite the spirit to feel its best.
Clouds drift softly in the azure sky,
As life around sings a lullaby.

In this haven of peace, we lose all care,
In the dance of meadows, joy fills the air.
The sun whispers secrets, the breeze sings along,
In the heart of the meadow, we truly belong.

Enchanted Wanderings at Dusk

As day surrenders to twilight's grace,
The world transforms in a soft embrace.
Shadows stretch long, the light starts to fade,
In enchanted wanderings, memories invade.

The whispers of night beckon with charm,
Guiding lost souls to a place warm.
Stars glimmer softly in the velvet sky,
Painting a canvas where dreams can fly.

Through winding paths and forest glades,
Where moonlight dances, and magic pervades.
A chorus of crickets breaks the calm,
In this tranquil hour, the heart feels the balm.

With every step, new wonders unfold,
In the twilight's arms, adventure is bold.
Through enchanted wanderings, we find our way,
In the dusk's soft glow, we wish not to stray.

Where Wildflowers Pulse with Laughter

In fields aglow, wildflowers sway,
Their laughter echoes at the close of day.
Colors bursting in joyous spree,
Nature's giggles, wild and free.

Beneath the sun, they dance and twirl,
Inviting dreams to unfurl.
Petals whisper secrets to the breeze,
Tickled by the playful tease.

Among the meadows, a vibrant song,
Carried by breezes, sweet and strong.
Bees hum along in blissful cheer,
In the land where joy draws near.

With each heartbeat, the wildflowers gleam,
Life's vivid canvas, a radiant dream.
In laughter's embrace, they gently sway,
A tapestry of colors in the fading day.

Reveries Under Starry Canopies

Beneath the vast celestial dome,
Dreams weave in the cosmic loam.
Whispers dance on a gentle breeze,
Crickets sing among the trees.

Night's fabric drapes the sleeping land,
Soft shadows where we gently stand.
Stars twinkle like eyes full of grace,
Glimmers of hope in dark's embrace.

The moon spills silver on the lake,
Reflections stir, as dreams awake.
In this realm where fantasies soar,
We lose ourselves forevermore.

With every sigh, the night unfolds,
Stories of ancients yet untold.
As dawn approaches, we softly part,
Leaving echoes within our heart.

The Melody of Wandering Spirits

In twilight's glow, the echoes play,
Spirits wandering fade away.
Their whispers in the autumn leaves,
A song of life that never grieves.

Between the shadows and the light,
They dance in dreams, a fleeting sight.
The melody guides their gentle flight,
A soft reminder of pure delight.

They swirl in circles, wild and free,
Lost in the notes of harmony.
Through fields of gold where silence reigns,
Their laughter lingers, sweet refrains.

As stars emerge in velvet skies,
Their serenade begins to rise.
An ethereal tune from dusk to dawn,
In nature's arms, forever drawn.

Meadows of Mist and Moonlight

In meadows draped in silver light,
Mist swirls softly, a haunting sight.
The moon caresses petals fair,
Whispers of night linger in the air.

Beneath the boughs of ancient trees,
The world is hushed, the heart at ease.
Crickets croon their serenades,
Where magic blooms and never fades.

The dance of shadows and soft glow,
Leads wandering souls where dreams will flow.
In every drop of dew that gleams,
Lie hidden tales and forgotten dreams.

As dawn awakens, day will rise,
But for a moment, night defies.
In meadows vast, the spirit flies,
Embracing wonder under the skies.

Chasing Butterflies in Twilight's Embrace

In twilight's glow, the colors blend,
Butterflies flit, with grace they send.
Underneath the twilight's sigh,
We chase their dreams, as time slips by.

Wings painted in hues of gold,
Stories of beauty yet untold.
Amidst the blooms where shadows dwell,
Each flutter casts a wistful spell.

Through gardens lush, we wander free,
In every flutter, a memory.
The laughter of youth ignites the air,
As magic dances, beyond compare.

With each small joy the heart regains,
A fleeting moment, no more chains.
In the embrace of fading light,
Chasing butterflies, a pure delight.